Foreword by the Chairman

Our north Norfolk town of Holt is very proud which stretches back to pre-Domesday. Today visit to the town will reveal the extensive Georgian influence, a result of rebuilding following a devastating fire in May 1708 which destroyed much of the town.

We are very fortunate to be able to understand and appreciate its Georgian history thanks to the contemporary diary of Mary Hardy. Mary lived in the next village from 1781 to 1809 and frequently visited Holt for work, shopping and recreation. This diary and the combined knowledge of historian Margaret Bird and the Holt Society have enabled this booklet to be written.

You, the reader, will be taken on a virtual walk, as shown on the copy of a Georgian map, around the town. The key buildings and landmarks will be outlined, along with their associated stories. These are supported by many photographs and explanations of the Georgian lifestyle at the time of Mary Hardy's diary, along with additional documents.

Reading about the sample market, the twice-yearly fair, how the many pubs 'underpinned a wide range of activities central to people's lives', along with the narrative on the local and regional justice system, gives a wonderfully rich description of life in Georgian Holt.

Throughout the booklet you will find revealing details surrounding the population of Holt at work, prayer and play; also the schooling of its children and the influence of war on its male inhabitants. However, the enormous contribution of the womenfolk is certainly not left out!

It is my hope, as Chairman of the Holt Society, that this booklet will not only be of interest to those who already know and love Holt. It will also inspire others to visit, enjoy and with the information contained in its pages appreciate this lovely town and its history.

KEITH GOSDEN, JP
Chairman, the Holt Society

February 2023

above **The Holt obelisk at the top of Letheringsett Hill greets those arriving from Norwich, Dereham and King's Lynn (page 32).**

It shows mileages to 28 places in Norfolk, accurate to early-19th-century road distances. Its image has become the logo of the Holt Society (facing page).
[*photo Margaret Bird 2011*]

front cover **This fine clock owned by Keith and Kate Gosden is the work of Francis Dusgate (d.1801 aged 77), a clockmaker and watchmaker at Holt.**

His skills with his hands were prized. He pulled out a troublesome tooth for Mary Hardy's husband William in 1787.
[*photo Keith Gosden 2022*]

MAP OF HOLT IN MARY HARDY'S TIME
Redrawn from Charles Burcham's Holt enclosure map of 1810 in the
National Archives [TNA: PRO MR 1/257, *detail*]. The shaded block
represents the extent of the built-up area, its street plan immediately
recognisable today. All around were fields, commons and heaths.
[*map Margaret Bird 2023*]

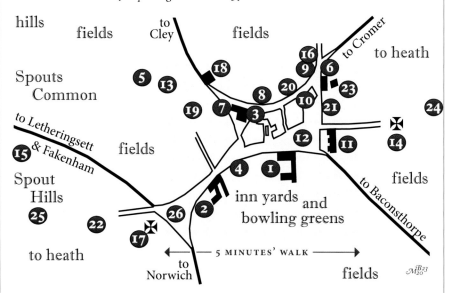

KEY   Places mentioned in the text, in the order in which they feature

1 Feathers	10 Dolphin	19 [Methodist Chapel 1838]
2 King's Head	11 Free Grammar School	20 Hanworth House 1744
3 Shirehouse	12 Market Place	21 Nelson House
4 'Manor House'	13 Windmill	22 Spout Hills
5 Fairstead	14 Parish Church	23 Playhouse
6 White Lion	15 Rectory	24 Workhouse
7 Black Boys	16 Quaker meeting house	25 The Frambeck
8 Bull	17 [Methodist Church 1863]	26 Obelisk
9 Angel	18 [Methodist Chapel 1813]	

Notes These 26 places are referenced in the text in red, eg [14],
their numbering reflecting the order in which they appear.
    The three Methodist chapels [17, 18 and 19] are included as
they feature in this booklet, although they were built after 1810.

1 · Holt's claims to prominence

This introduction to the people of Holt and the forces shaping local society in the period 1780–1810 began life as walking tours for the Holt Society.[1] In recent years a series of well-illustrated studies of the town's buildings and landmarks has been published.[2] This one aims to be different. It features daily life, work and play as experienced by the townsfolk. We even have a glimpse of what it was like to be a child at school in Holt (in chapter 5).

Given the nature of the contemporary sources, such insights are not usually possible. We are lucky to have an eye-witness: the diarist Mary Hardy (1733–1809); she lived nearby at Letheringsett Hall, in the Glaven valley, from 1781. Born at Whissonsett in central Norfolk, she kept a daily diary for nearly 36 years until her death. She or members of her family visited Holt almost every day, giving a vivid picture of the town's commercial life, services and leisure opportunities. The Hardys valued Holt for the stimulus and sociability it provided as they pursued a very active working life as farmers, maltsters, brewers and owners of a large portfolio of public houses.

[1] *tours* An 'indoor tour' for the Society's members in March 2022 was followed by two walking tours in July 2022 as part of the Holt Festival. All were led by Margaret Bird.

[2] *buildings* See Steve Benson's *A Stroll through Georgian Holt* (2004, revised 2017); the leaflet *Welcome to the Holt Owl Trail* (2019, free, from local outlets); and Mary Alexander's *First Impressions* (2011, revised 2022).

The Owl Trail and the 30-minute film *A Stroll through Georgian Holt*, featuring Steve Benson, are available on the Holt Society website: www.theholtsociety.org

left Baker's store at Holt in 1919. It faces today's Byfords, between the High Street and Shirehall Plain, and is currently an estate agent's premises.

From a shopkeeping family herself, Mary Hardy was very much at ease in retailers' company. Baker's shop in her time was an ironmongery, and had not yet expanded into other lines.

[NRO: MC 2043/2/135, 908 x 8, *Checkley Collection*]

It is significant that a very hardworking woman should be our chief guide, for Holt relied on the contribution made by working women to its prosperity (chapter 4).

above The Feathers was Holt's premier coaching inn. Like other public houses it hosted the sample market in grain where farmers, maltsters and millers bargained into the small hours.
[*photo Margaret Bird 2011*]

1 *manors* The proceedings of the manor courts were noted in the manor court books, now held in the Norfolk Record Office (NRO).

Those for Holt Pereers were compiled for the lords of the manor—the Fishmongers' Company, a livery company in the City of London and trustees for the Free Grammar School (later Gresham's School): NRO: MC 2987.

The other court books have the reference ACC Cozens-Hardy 20/3/1973.

What made Holt special in the late eighteenth century? Five key features helped to create a remarkably vibrant community and raised it to prominence among the county's 27 market towns. These factors will be described in greater detail, but can be summarised here:

◆ A vigorous sample market in grain was conducted inside its leading inns on market day: inns such as the Feathers [1] and King's Head [2]. Huge sums of money would be involved as farmers and manufacturers concluded deals over the sale and purchase of barley for malting and wheat for milling; as much as £80 and £100 might be at stake in any single transaction. The stalls for the pitched market, while marking a more visible aspect of Holt's trade, by contrast witnessed paltry sums of money changing hands and formed an inconsiderable element in establishing the town's reputation.

◆ Only four towns in Norfolk hosted the county quarter sessions by adjournment, in addition to the provincial capital, Norwich, which served as the main seat of justice at quarter sessions level. Holt hosted the sessions in October and January, while Walsingham held them in April and July. King's Lynn and Swaffham also alternated, serving the west of the county. As a result, those seeking remedies were within reach of the magistrates and did not have to journey to Norwich. (Great Yarmouth had its own judicial system.) Thus the Shirehouse [3], as it was then known, signalled difference. Its presence elevated Holt above its local competitors.

◆ The town had four manors: Holt, Holt Market, Holt Hales and Holt Pereers.[1] Manor courts oversaw conveyancing of copyhold property, which was then a common method of property-holding and enabled copyholders to devise their lands and buildings as they chose. Crucially, women could control their property and leave it to their children or others of their choice without interference from their husbands or parents. Whereas common law and statute law restricted women's property rights, the manor courts, like the church courts, respected female sovereignty and ensured their independence. With four manors in the town, meeting in their respective manor houses [4], the lawyers would have been kept busy over such matters as house purchases and sales, mortgages and wills. Through the court records we can also trace the tying of public houses by wholesale brewers like the Hardys as they secured an outlet by copyhold ownership.

◆ Britain was at war almost continuously between 1775 and 1815. In certain periods invasion by the French was greatly feared even as far north as Norfolk, for France annexed the Austrian Netherlands (today's Belgium) in 1794 and the United Provinces (today's Holland) in 1795.

This control of a long seaboard gave them a launching pad for the invasion of East Anglia—including north Norfolk. London decreed that Holt should serve as the counter-invasion military hub for the northern half of Norfolk. As a consequence the town, with its surrounding area, was flooded with troops who all had to be billeted when they were not encamped at Weybourne.

◆ Lastly, Holt hosted a large fair twice a year, on 25 April and 25 November. This was not some trivial event in the local calendar, but a major horse and cattle fair in the morning followed by a general fair for the rest of the day and into the night and next day. Others nearby, such as Cley and Weybourne, had seen their fairs decline to little more than a few stalls for haberdashery and trinkets, but Holt Fair still attracted large crowds in this period. It was held on the open space called the Fairstead [5], at the far end of what became Withers Street (today's New Street).

Any notion of the presence of genteel, leisured townsfolk needs to be dispelled early. Holt was defined by work and working people, and this story begins with them.

above **The Shirehouse, now called the Shirehall, gave Holt the status of a leading county town.**

Only three others, apart from Norwich, hosted the Norfolk quarter sessions which drew large numbers four times a year.
[*photo Margaret Bird 2011*]

above **A handsome doorcase for a house traditionally known as the 'Manor House', in the High Street.**

But which of the four manors did it serve?
[*photo Margaret Bird 2011*]

2 · The town at work

¹ *directory* Local people, usually clergy, would send in copy for the massive work. The 2½-page entry for Holt, on pages 279–81 of volume 3, also covers many nearby small towns and villages.

² *Laviles* One of Letheringsett's manors, covering the lands east of the River Glaven.

below right The ledger stone under the altar in **Holt Church to Edmund Jewell (d.1784 aged 65) and his wife Sarah (d.1794).**

They stood at the pinnacle of Holt society. Edmund, an attorney, was the Chairman of Quarter Sessions and commanding officer of the Holt and Letheringsett Volunteers.

This unit was formed in early 1781 near the end of the American war, when a landing by the Dutch was feared. His former troops formed a guard of honour at his funeral—an event held in pouring rain, as Mary Hardy records.

Sarah Jewell was one of only four heads of household listed as Holt gentry in the *Universal British Directory*, volume 3 (1794). [*photo Margaret Bird 2022*]

The nation's earliest trade directory, the *Universal British Directory*, published in five volumes 1793–98, reveals that Holt was then far from gentrified.[1] In fact only four heads of household are classed as gentry in a town of 180 houses—this last figure being given by the rector in 1784 in his report to the bishop (see page 17). One of the four was James Hewitt, absentee lord of the manor of Letheringsett Laviles;[2] his son, the Holt attorney Charles Hewitt, served as commanding officer of the Holt Volunteer Infantry at the start of the Napoleonic War (page 29).

The widowed Sarah Jewell is listed as gentry, as is Thomas Fisher, who had recently moved to Holt after farming at nearby Sharrington Hall. The fourth, Thomas Bensley, lived at Holt for only a few years. All feature in Mary Hardy's diary in the 1780s and 1790s, even though she and her family had no claim to gentry status at that time. Her record shows us that easy mixing across the classes was a marked characteristic of Norfolk life.

The directory names other leading townsfolk: two clergymen, four surgeons, three attorneys and 33 men and women in trade. This list merely touches the surface,

left The King's Head on the High Street is decked out for Queen Elizabeth's Diamond Jubilee. [*photo Christopher Bird 2012*]

below A warming pan at the Feathers, its hot coals used for airing beds. The pans could be dangerous. One burned the leg of two-year-old Mary Ann Hardy. [*photo Margaret Bird 2011*]

for only two innkeepers are deemed worthy of mention—those at the Feathers and White Lion [6]. The other seven are omitted, as also tradesmen and women in a small way and working wives engaged in such various roles as handspinners, dressmakers and washerwomen. Everyone in Holt apart from the gentry was a worker.

One name will be familiar to shoppers in Holt today: the churchwarden John Baker (1727–1804), formerly of Wells, who had joined the ironmongery business of his father-in-law Adam Custance in 1770. His family were friends of the Hardys, his second wife Priscilla being related by marriage to the diarist. As seen on page 14, the Baker name was not especially prominent then, being just one of many retailers trading in the town centre.

Running the public houses

No discussion of the world of work in the eighteenth century can continue long without a look at the public houses. They underpinned a wide range of activities central to people's lives, being associated with work, local administration, transport and leisure as well as drinking.

In 1801 Holt had 1004 inhabitants and nine public houses: a ratio of one outlet for every 112 persons. High

right The colourful inn board at the former White Lion. This inn at the start of the Cromer road stood at the north-east extremity of the built-up area.

As was common, it suffered rapid turnover among its innkeepers. Richard Dobson, John Bullock, John Howard and James William Skiffins in turn were in charge 1781–1808.

A sale notice in the *Norwich Mercury* for 24 March 1798 stated it had two kitchens, a large bar, two parlours, a large dining room, eight bedrooms and a bowling green. [*photo Margaret Bird 2011*]

[1] *ratios* These calculations are made by dividing the population in the 1801 national census by the number of outlets as listed in the alehousekeepers' recognisances in the Norfolk Record Office for 1789–99 (NRO: C/Sch 1/16).

numbers of licensed premises were a common feature of market towns as they served far more than the resident population. The surrounding countryside too did well. The ratio for Holt hundred, a wide administrative area across north Norfolk containing 26 towns and villages and a total population of 7500 persons, was 1:183.[1]

This represented very generous drinking provision. In general, Norfolk's magistrates took a relaxed view over issuing public-house licenses and did not favour suppression of outlets even in the turbulent political times of the 1790s when it was feared that public houses might serve as breeding grounds for sedition and civil unrest.

Before looking at the role the public houses played we need to establish the way they were run. Larger ones like the Feathers, White Lion and King's Head at Holt were classed as inns as they offered meals, good stabling and overnight accommodation. Smaller ones, often sited away from the main thoroughfares, such as the Black Boys [7] and the Bull [8], were classed as alehouses.

Holt's suffered the same fate as others in the county: the innkeepers found it hard to make a living from the trade and often did not last long in post. The Black Boys, for instance, built against the west wall of the Shirehouse, had as many as *eight* innkeepers 1781–1808, one of whom served for two terms. Even prominent inns faced problems of fairly high turnover, the Feathers and the King's Head each having five tenants in a thirty-year period.

left The site of the Black Boys, a small public house which adjoined the Shirehouse seen here on the right. In 1783 Raven Hardy became the copyholder (the owner), aged 16. It suffered very high innkeeping turnover, and had closed by about 1830.

It was then rebuilt by William Hardy jnr and became a manse for the Methodist minister. The brewer's nephew and heir William Hardy Cozens-Hardy remodelled it as seen here, as a manse for the breakaway Methodist movement he championed from 1850, the Wesleyan Reformers.
[*photo Margaret Bird 2022*]

There was a reason for this. The common brewers, as the wholesalers were called, had a stranglehold over the public houses through the process of tying.[1] As brewers' fortunes rose and fell they traded their outlets with remarkable rapidity, causing instability for their tenants. When Back's Brewery twelve miles away at Cawston was struggling in late 1783 it put its Holt outlet, the Black Boys, up for sale. William Hardy, newly arrived at Letheringsett from Coltishall on the Norfolk Broads, snapped it up for his elder son Raven (1767–87), then aged only sixteen; Raven was Mary Hardy's maiden name. The purchase price was 100 guineas (£105), at the low end of public-house property values.[2]

William Hardy and later his younger son William Hardy junior (1770–1842) held a string of outlets across a 25-mile radius; their most distant outpost lay at Stalham near the coast. During 1781–1810 their Letheringsett brewery supplied seven of Holt's nine public houses, four of these additionally being secured by tie. The map on page 2 locates all seven, including the Angel [9] and the Dolphin [10], (later called the Star). The location of the two which escaped the Hardys' attentions, the Phoenix and the Mariners, is not known.

[1] *tying* The term had the same meaning as today. The brewer secured the outlet by purchase, by renting it or by controlling the innkeeper through a mortgage or bond; the outlet had to sell the brewer's beers.

[2] *Black Boys* It was a very modest alehouse, as we learn from the manor court book. It comprised 'one cottage to west of Shirehouse in Holt and land formerly waste [common land] and a stable' (NRO: ACC Cozens-Hardy 20/3/1973).

above The diarist's son, the talented Letheringsett maltster, brewer and estate owner William Hardy jnr, aged about 56; the artist is unknown.

He left his mark on Holt's pubs and Methodist chapels, and supervised the running of the Free Grammar School (later Gresham's) as a 'visitor'. [*Cozens-Hardy Collection*]

[1] *petty sessions* Held weekly for lesser matters, eg swearing in Militia recruits, confirming the election of parish officers (such as overseers of the poor), sorting problems of vagrancy, and unmarried mothers' paternity cases.

Quarter sessions had greater powers (pages 14–15).

Only 29 per cent of the innkeepers at ninety of the Hardys' public houses in 1789 were still at the same outlet ten years later. Illiquidity, debt and bankruptcy cast a shadow over the innkeepers' lives. Henry Crafer at the King's Head became bankrupt in 1796, causing problems for his brewer to whom he owed large debts. In that same year William Bulling's debts at the Bull (in Bull Street) had spiralled out of control. To pay off William Hardy he surrendered his small farm on Holt Heath to the brewer. Some of this land north of the Cromer road was sold by the Cozens-Hardys over a century later and became part of Gresham's School on its new site.

Life could get even harder for publicans at the mercy of a wholesale brewer. During the 36 years of Mary Hardy's diary we learn that William Hardy senior and junior consigned seven of their tenants to the debtors' prison at Norwich Castle, as the unfortunate men were unable to repay their debts.

Given this harsh financial climate, the way the hardworking men and women who ran the public houses managed to provide a useful range of services is a remarkable tribute to their resilience. The inns helped drive the local economy as they hosted the sample market in grain—the unseen world described in the next section. They also gave support to a mass of local administration as petty sessions could be held there as well as in the Shirehouse. These included hiring sessions for servants working on the land as well as in private homes, and annual licensing sessions for public houses.[1] Justices of the peace would dine at the inns afterwards, often in the company of brewers like William Hardy.

The inns hosted school feasts, including the annual feast of Holt's Free Grammar School [11] in December. Tithe frolics (festive feasts), bowling clubs and their frolics (three of Holt's inns had bowling greens), book clubs, music clubs and masonic lodges: all were based at the public houses, which also provided venues for balls. In addition, the hardpressed innkeepers had to cope

with billeted troops (as seen on page 28) and with offering postchaise services. Some public houses hired out their own vehicles, while others just provided refreshment for passengers and horses on their journeys. Horses could not be driven for more than twelve miles without taking a break or being changed.[1]

The hidden world of the sample market

Every settlement in rural areas needed to be within roughly twelve miles of a market town. Market over-supply would hurt the viability of an individual town's economy; under-supply would deny villagers moderately easy access to these vital places of exchange. Holt lay comfortably twelve miles from Aylsham and Fakenham and fifteen from North Walsham, at the heart of a great agricultural countryside.[2] Then, as now, Norfolk and Suffolk formed the nation's prime arable region.

To suit everyone's convenience market days were staggered, enabling buyers and sellers to do business in more than one town. Saturday was market day for Holt and Norwich, Thursday for Fakenham and North Walsham, and Tuesday for the more modest market at Aylsham.[3]

[1] *postchaises* Coaches and postchaises broke their 21-mile journey to Norwich at the Woodrow Inn, Cawston. The landmark building still stands on the main road, beside a garage.

[2] *Holt's market* Its charter had been granted by King Edward II in 1309. However an earlier market had existed, one of very few named in Norfolk's Domesday (the post-Conquest survey of 1086).

[3] *market towns* The 1801 populations varied. Holt and Little Walsingham (insignificant as a market) each had 1004. Fakenham had 1236, Aylsham 1667 and North Walsham 1959.

¹ *Fakenham, Holt, North Walsham* These markets are described in detail, with comparisons and contemporary accounts, in M. Bird, *Mary Hardy and her World* (2020), vol. 3, pp. 513–40.

above The memorial in Blakeney churchyard, four miles from Holt, to the merchant Henry Smith, who died aged 32 during the night of 24–25 May 1794 on his way home from Holt market. His posthumous son James is also commemorated.

He fell from his horse having left Holt at 2 am, according to Mary Hardy. He then drowned in Cley Watering, the stream which crosses the Holt–Cley road. The night-time sample market posed special dangers.

[*photo Margaret Bird 2000*]

Fakenham had the greatest corn market in Britain by 1804; its competitors at Holt, North Walsham and Norwich were also very significant players.¹ As explained on page 4, Holt's market in fact operated across the town and not just in the Market Place [12] which was set aside for the stalls—the pitched market. The sample market was conducted unseen at inns stretching from near the High Street's west end to the start of the Cromer road.

Founded on trust alone, it was governed by the long-held pledge, 'My word is my bond.' Suppliers (the farmers) would arrive from mid-afternoon on market day and trade long into the night. They carried little pouches of grain, and would spill the contents into the palm of their hand to be inspected by the purchasers: cornmillers, maltsters and brewers. The bulk produce in any subsequent deal had always to match the quality of the sample, otherwise that trader would be banned for the future and his reputation shattered.

It was an extremely efficient system. Foodstuffs for the pitched market had to be transported for miles to the point of exchange and then transported once more to the buyer's premises. However there was no need to take cartloads or wagonloads of grain to the inns as the produce went direct to the purchaser. This not only reduced costs, for bulk carriage was expensive, but saved the grain from being exposed unnecessarily to the elements.

Middlemen attended the sample market too: factors for the sellers, and merchants for the buyers. Trading was intense and prolonged, Mary Hardy regularly recording her husband getting home from local markets in the small hours or even early morning. Riding in the dark presented very real dangers, especially if large amounts of drink had lubricated negotiations. The Blakeney merchant Henry Smith fell off his horse and drowned when returning home. The inquest heard a poignant piece of evidence: 'His dog, which lay by him when found, had torn his hat in pieces in endeavouring to pull him out of the water' (*Norwich Mercury*, 31 May 1794).

left **Holt's brick tower mill of 1794 seen in 1916 before its sails were removed in 1925; it was finally demolished in 1974.**

In 1786 the Letheringsett farmer (and later Holt auctioneer) Charles Kendle had built a mill here on the large fairstead. On 30 June 1792 a notice in the *Norwich Mercury* stated its round house could store 20 lasts of corn (200 quarters), so this mill's predecessor was a post mill: smock mills and tower mills do not have round houses.

The Hardys' friend John Wade was the working miller, as Kendle's tenant, when the mill burned down in four hours in May 1794. Friction from the stones had set it alight. The loss broke Kendle.
[NRO: MC 2043/9, 909x6, *Checkley Collection*]

[1] *malting* Norfolk was the nation's foremost producer of brewing malt. Huge shiploads passed through Wells, with the twin ports of Blakeney and Cley handling smaller consignments.

Holt had no commercial brewery. As explained on page 30, the town lacked a good water supply. The Hardys' well-equipped concern on the main road at Letheringsett was the nearest brewery.

Cornmilling and retailing

Little manufacturing took place in Holt. Malting, both then and now a major Norfolk industry, had long been carried out nearby beside the River Glaven at Letheringsett and Cley.[1] That same river powered a series of corn watermills which in 1786 found themselves facing competition at Holt. The Hardys walked up to the fairstead that summer to see 'the new mill', built by Charles Kendle. It had a short life. On 8 May 1794 it burned down in four

[1] *four hours* The Hardys' brewery appentice Henry Raven (1777–1825) is our only source for this statement. He kept a diary which is published alongside his aunt's (M. Bird, ed., *The Diary of Mary Hardy 1773–1809* (2013), Diary 3, 8 May 1794).

[2] *Nîmes* Diary 2, 31 August 1788.

Nîmes is famous as the birthplace of the tough fabric denim, its name being a corruption of 'de Nîmes'.

hours in a high wind and the whole stock of flour was lost.[1] Post mills are built of timber; this mill's five-floored successor was prudently built of brick [13].

A feature of all market towns was their range of shops: grocers, drapers, tailors, chandlers selling candles, ironmongers, printers and milliners. Holt was no exception, and we learn a great deal about its retailers from Mary Hardy—herself from a family of grocers and drapers. While most villages in East Anglia had a shop offering basic necessities such as tea, sugar, flour, spices and candles, towns catered for more specialist requirements.

The churchwarden John Davy (d.1805 aged 69 or 70) and Charles Sales (d.1821 aged 68) were Holt's leading grocers with the most prominent establishments; they were also drapers. Grocers possessed an outlook which reached far beyond the confines of their town and surrounding area. They had to be aware of restrictions on trade caused by war, and of hurricanes and earthquakes overseas which would seriously damage the supply of everyday goods such as sugar. These international topics would be fully covered in the Norwich newspapers.

Many shopkeepers would apprentice their teenage children, both boys and girls, away from home. John Davy's son John settled as a grocer in the City of London, and Davy's daughter Ann became a millinery apprentice at Woodbridge, Suffolk. Having trained in London as a linen draper their brother Edward toured abroad as a travelling agent for his London firm. Ned Davy died young at Nîmes, a textile centre in the south of France.[2]

above The Letheringsett brewer William Hardy (1732–1811) served on grand and petty juries at Holt. Jurors were drawn from across the villages of north-east Norfolk as well as from the town itself. [*portrait by Huguier 1785: Cozens-Hardy Collection*]

Administering justice

The significance of Holt's role as a seat of justice, outlined on page 4, cannot be over-emphasised. Holding the quarter sessions brought large numbers of litigants to the town from across north-east Norfolk. The Shirehouse hosted the second highest court in the county after the assizes, which were held at Thetford every March and in Norwich every July. Quarter sessions could not hear capital cases, which were referred to the assizes presided over by judges, but quarter sessions magistrates heard all other criminal and civil lawsuits. Male ratepayers from towns and villages across a wide area would sit on two types of jury: the petty jury, akin to today's jury which determines whether the defendant is guilty, and the grand jury, which would consider whether sufficient evidence existed to merit bringing a case.[1]

It is sometimes thought that gallows could be found in the countryside, but by the eighteenth century this was no longer the case; it is likely gallows are being confused with gibbets. In Norfolk all executions had to be conducted publicly outside Norwich Castle. Occasionally the bodies of the hanged were exhibited on gibbets near the scene of the crime.[2] As discussed in volume 3 of *Mary Hardy and her World*, it could not be said that a Bloody Code was imposed in Norfolk in Mary Hardy's time. Justice was tempered with mercy, and the majority of those facing death had their sentences commuted. At quarter sessions level the records show that justices of the peace knew 'the temper of the inhabitants', to use a phrase then common; temper equates to temperament. They lived among them, and understood the pressures on them. Out of session the solemn courthouse witnessed festivities, for the Shirehouse hosted organ concerts and Holt's monthly winter balls called assemblies.

[1] *grand jury* Its role was abolished in England and Wales in 1933, but it is retained in the United States. William Hardy and his son often sat on both types of jury at Holt.

Grand juries, relying on their local knowledge of the parties and the causes, would throw out a case if they thought it vexacious or unconvincing.

Quarter sessions were abolished in 1972 after nearly six centuries of continuous history. Their functions, and those of the assizes, were amalgamated in the new crown courts.

[2] *hangings* In the 1770s the Hardys would take their very young children to watch executions, as part of their education. Once the parents made a detour near Fakenham to see the corpse of a newly hanged man gibbeted on Kettlestone Common (Diary 2, 14 April 1792).

left The parish church in the early 20th century, from a postcard; the north gallery is still in place. The 13th-century font survived the great fire of 1 May 1708 which destroyed much of Holt and the church's interior.
[*photo by the Preston Brothers*]

right The west front of St
Andrew's Church, Holt is
now approached by an
avenue of limes.

According to M.J. Arm-
strong in his *History and
Antiquities of the County of
Norfolk* (1781), the tower
was surmounted by a high
spire until its destruction
in the 1708 fire. It had
served as a prominent
seamark for sailors.
[*photo Margaret Bird 2022*]

below The Revd George
Barrs (1771–1840) was for
40 years Curate of Rowley
Regis, a very deprived area
west of Birmingham.

A fiery gospel-preacher,
he served in Norfolk 1799–
1800 after his Cambridge
graduation and ordination
at Ely. Mary Hardy first
heard him preach at Holt
and then followed him
around north Norfolk's
Evangelical circuit.
[*by Thomas Kirby 1820:
photo Matthew Shelton
of Rowley Regis 2012*]

3 · The town at prayer

The diocese of Norwich in this period is popularly characterised as 'the Dead See'. Nothing could be further
from the truth. Holt was one of a large number of areas
across Norfolk witnessing an intense religious revival
within the Church of England and a flurry of Nonconformist cottage meetings; the Methodists in particular
were on the march. The active sermon-taster Mary Hardy
is sometimes our sole source noting these developments.

St Andrew's: 'The church was crowded'

Holt Church [14] was served for 54 years by its resident rector, the Revd Joshua Smith (1725–1804), assisted by a series of curates. His large rectory [15] still stands on the main road halfway down Letheringsett Hill, to the west of the town. Mr Smith was lord of the manor of three of Holt's manors: Holt, Holt Market and Holt Hales.[1]

As was common in Norfolk and Norwich, the main service on a Sunday, with a sermon, was held in the afternoon or early evening. The long-hours culture then prevalent meant that Sunday morning was usually set aside for business and work, as in the Hardy household. Holt's townsfolk had a particular reason for preferring the afternoon as market trading the previous day would have continued far into the night.

Religious restlessness characterised churchgoing and chapel-going at this time, with little family cohesion over worship. From Mary Hardy's record it is clear that individual members of a family would shop around in the search for spiritual fulfilment. The diarist and her daughter rarely attended Holt Church, whereas William Hardy and his son were often there for the afternoon service. Conversely, Holt people would sometimes go down the hill to Letheringsett Church on a Sunday.

In his report to the new Bishop of Norwich in 1784 the rector stated that at his three Communion services a year he had forty communicants in a town with 180 houses.[2] We can guess from the 1801 census that it had nearly 1000 people in the 1780s, producing a four-per-cent participation rate. However such fairly low percentages at Communion were widespread other than in estate villages dominated by a single landowner enforcing attendance.

All this was to change. The tolerant rector welcomed Evangelicals into his pulpit from 1799, many trained by the famous Revd Charles Simeon of Cambridge. The first to arrive was the theatrical George Barrs, whom Mary Hardy rated as 'excellent'. At his last performance 'the church was crowded.'[3]

below **Detail of the church font, with its unusual swags of fleurs-de-lys.**

Most unusually for north Norfolk the clergy noted only baptisms at the font and not the private ceremony within a day or two of birth, as was the norm.

Since parents let their offspring accumulate before bringing them to the church ceremony, to save on christening party costs, the registers suggest improbably high numbers of twins and triplets.

[*photo Margaret Bird 2022*]

1 *three manors* See the notes on pages 4 and 22; also pages 20–21 for the way manorial customary law empowered women.

2 *report* NRO: DN/VIS 29/6, Holt deanery visitation.

3 *crowded* Diary 4, 18 August 1799.

The Methodists get a violent reception

Religious Nonconformity came to Holt long before the Methodist chapels were built. The Quakers had a meeting house [16] opposite the White Lion. It would have been supported by those in the wider area, as the rector told the bishop in 1784 and 1794 that Holt had only one Quaker in the parish. The town also had two families of Independents (later to become the Congregationalists).

The first Methodists to arrive were not the followers of John Wesley. They adhered to a different strand of Methodism led by the Revd George Whitefield (1714–70) and Selina, Countess of Huntingdon (1707–91). As early as 1757 the Briston attorney, schoolmaster and money-lender Thomas Mendham (d.1793 aged 58) had started registering private houses, barns and industrial buildings across north Norfolk for worship outside the Church of England. He chose Holt for the first of sixteen such meetings. By 1780 these Calvinistic Methodists were holding their meetings in a barn at the Feathers.

Mendham's efforts were violently resisted by some in Holt. Mary Hardy relates that his followers had to face 'a mob' in the summer of 1783, some of the rioters being taken into custody. Eighty years later her grandson William Hardy Cozens-Hardy (1806–95) recalled those stirring events as he laid the foundation stone of the 1863 Methodist Church [17]. Built on his land, and largely at his expense, it still stands facing Obelisk Plain. The mob of 1783, he said, seized the pulpit in use in the Methodist meeting and placed it on the town pump. He may have heard the tale from his uncle William Hardy junior, who was thirteen years old at the time.[1]

The Wesleyan Methodists did not establish a place of worship in Holt until 1790, in the house of the tailor John Mason. Under the vigorous leadership and financial sponsorship of William Hardy junior the Wesleyans at last gained a purpose-built chapel in 1813 later named Chancery Buildings [18]. This became the British School, for Nonconformists, when the 1838 chapel opened [19].

1 *Mendham's meetings*
The story of the Calvinistic Methodists is told in *Mary Hardy and her World*, vol. 3, pp. 183–207. The Wesleyans are chronicled on pp. 207–38.
    The registration records for the meetings under the Toleration Act are held in the NRO: DN/DIS 1/2.

left The first purpose-built Methodist chapel in Holt faces the burial ground of the second chapel. Like its successor it bears the architectural hallmarks of William Mindham (1771–1843), of Holt, who worked for William Hardy jnr throughout his career. [*photo Margaret Bird 2022*]

below Holt Methodist Church was built by Mary Hardy's grandson when he led the Wesleyan Reformers, a breakaway group from the Wesleyan Methodists. [*Cozens-Hardy Collection*]

Two women played a crucial role in shaping Holt's Methodism: Mary Hardy and her daughter Mary Ann (1773–1864).[1] Mary Ann's only son William Hardy Cozens-Hardy adopted his mother's allegiance (Wesleyan, later Wesleyan Reformer) and not his father's, which was Baptist. Like her brother, Mary Ann financed Wesleyan chapels in Norwich; William Hardy junior also helped to establish them in other parts of the county.

facing page The front and rear of the 1838 Wesleyan Methodist chapel in New Street.

The rear elevation closely resembles the style of the early-19th-century malt-kilns and tun room at Letheringsett designed by William Mindham. [*photos Margaret Bird 2022*]

Their father the brewer was never a Nonconformist, remaining a staunch Anglican all his days. It was Mary Hardy's profound influence over her children which led to their promotion of Methodism. This phenomenon brings us to the role of women more generally, whose contribution is so often neglected in the historical record.

4 · Women to the fore

It is often assumed that women had few rights in the days before the Married Women's Property Acts of 1870 and 1882 which ensured that wives could have control

[1] *Mary Hardy* She was 'double-minded': both Anglican and Methodist

above The Feathers, facing north onto the Market Place. Its official name in the 18th century was the Three Feathers, the emblem of the Prince of Wales seen above the door on the right.

It was run 1780–94 by the widowed Elizabeth Sheppard, probably the most prominent woman in the town and member of the commercial elite.
[*photo Margaret Bird 1992*]

over their own income, property and assets. This was far from the case. Many married women at Holt were forceful personalities in our period and treated by their husbands as valued partners in business enterprises, as was the case with Mary Hardy herself. Instances of the respect and trust in which women were held took many forms.

Firstly the law specifically recognised the separate legal identity of a woman from that of her spouse. Manorial law operated at Holt and in Norfolk generally. In the manor courts, as also in church courts, women (married, single and widowed) could appear on their own behalf and argue their case themselves. Manorial law rejected 'coverture': the principle that a wife's identity was subsumed into that of her husband, as represented by her adoption of his surname on marriage. Coverture held sway under common law and statute law, resulting in a married female innkeeper being debarred from becoming the licensee as the sector was governed by statute law. However under manorial custom a wife could devise her own property as she wished; she could also own it in her own right.[1] We see these rights being exercised on a regular basis in Mary Hardy's circle.

Holt had a large number of working women like the harnessmaker Philippa Basham (d.1846 aged 84), the innkeeper Elizabeth Sheppard (d.1816 aged 77) and dressmakers and milliners. Luke Basham had been killed aged 38 in a fall from his horse in 1801, but his energetic widow carried on his High Street business for 45 years for the benefit of their children, some of whom succeeded her. She was still in charge by the time of White's 1845 county directory, where she is named as a saddler.

It was very common for husbands to write in admiration of their wives' abilities when appointing them executors of their wills. It is evident from the language used that wives regularly participated in their spouses' trade or concern. Mary Davy (d.1820 aged 80), herself from a family of grocers at Cawston, took over her husband's grocery and drapery at Holt on his death in 1805.

The outstanding example is that of Mrs Sheppard. She and her husband John were followers of Thomas Mendham, which probably explains why the Feathers' barn was used for Methodist meetings. John died in 1780 leaving Elizabeth with young children, yet she courageously took on all the responsibilities of running this busy coaching inn which also served as the town's post office.

She definitely had presence, for Parson Woodforde referred to her by name on staying overnight at her inn when passing through Holt. The clerical diarist from Weston in central Norfolk noted on 11 September 1787: 'Took a ride to Holt . . . and there we supped and slept at the Feathers Inn, kept by a Mrs Shepherd. Holt stands well, and [is] a good decent town.'

She was prepared to be innovative. In 1784 she promoted a private transport service, paid for by subscription. The stage coach would run from Wells to Norwich via Holt and Aylsham, Mary Hardy becoming one of the subscribers. Women were accustomed to travelling with-

above The prolific diarist Mary Hardy, née Raven.

Her 500,000-word text with its precise record of life in the Holt area is an amazing achievement, for she was not a woman of leisure. She actively helped in the family's diversified business. [*portrait by Huguier 1785: Cozens-Hardy Collection*]

[1] *manor courts* Held at the manor house, with the court steward acting for the lord or lady of the manor in their absence, courts often merely confirmed what had already been agreed out of court at a lawyer's house.

Manors were areas of land comprising built-up areas, farms, commons and heaths. They had Saxon and early-mediaeval origins.

[1] *Mrs Sheppard* For her coach service see the second volume of the Diary and the *Norwich Mercury*, 4 December 1784. She advertised her post-chaise service in the same paper on 16 April 1791.

She succeeded her late husband as excise office-keeper (The National Archives: PRO CUST 47/322, p. 58, 26 October 1780).

[2] *Sophia Burcham* Diary 2, 16 July and 22 July 1787.

This was the pre-Jenner method called variolation. Patients often lived in the surgeon's household while undergoing treatment.

[3] *T.W. Coke* His father Wenman Roberts (d.1776) changed his surname to Coke in 1750 in order to secure Holkham for himself and his descendants.

[4] *Joshua Smith* The story is complicated. On Revd Dr Briggs' death his 16-year-old daughter Elizabeth (d.1810 aged 79) inherited the advowson (the right of appointing the rector) from him. She soon chose her betrothed as the new parson.

She also gave Joshua Smith the lordship of the three manors which had been her father's (L.B. Radford, *History of Holt* (1908), pp. 68, 76–7).

out their menfolk, and this private service may have been reassuring for female passengers.

It is a mark of Mrs Sheppard's standing that she helped with tax collection—a function usually regarded as a male preserve. The excise service in London treated female innkeepers on an equal footing with their male counter-parts. Mrs Sheppard was appointed excise officekeeper during the whole of her tenure at Holt, requiring her to collect and store securely the excise duty paid by manu-facturers such as maltsters, brewers and tanners. Very large sums of money were involved, each payment being perhaps £90 or £100 or more, yet women were trusted to have a formal role in the workings of the fiscal state.[1]

From 1786 women were at the forefront of the new Sunday School movement within the Church of England. Sarah Bartell (d.1828 aged 82), wife of the Holt surgeon-apothecary Edmund Bartell (d.1816 aged 72), helped run the Holt school. She worked closely with Mary Hardy, busy with the Letheringsett school, and the two women journeyed to Norwich to trawl the city schools for ideas.

Mrs Bartell (the name was pronounced Bartle) was already at full stretch with her husband's work. One of her tasks was to nurse children through smallpox inocu-lation; at times she had to cope with distressing out-comes, for the old method was dangerous. Eleven-year-old Sophia Burcham, the daughter of an East Dereham surveyor and valuer, died while under the Bartells' care.[2]

Lastly, one obvious female role can be overlooked. Women served as channels by which wealth, inheritance and title to property were passed on. The Hardy line con-tinued only through Mary Ann's marriage to Jeremiah Cozens in 1805. Thomas William Coke, famous as Coke of Norfolk, owed his Holkham inheritance to his grand-mother Anne Coke, who had married Philip Roberts.[3]

The Rector of Holt in our period gained his position and impressive home through marriage. Joshua Smith's wife was Elizabeth, daughter of an earlier rector Dr Henry Briggs (1687–1748), for 26 years rector of Holt.[4]

5 · Children's schooldays

HOLT SCHOOL, NORFOLK; FORMERLY THE RESIDENCE OF THE GRESHAM FAMILY.
From a sketch made on the spot in 1838.

left **Holt's Free Grammar School as it looked in 1838, from an unsigned sketch.**
[*Gresham's School Archive, ref. 2015.4*]

One of Holt's principal assets was its free grammar school, set prominently in the town centre. Founded in 1554, it was free in the sense that up to thirty boys at any one time could be taught 'on the foundation'—thereby giving the children of the poor a valuable educational opportunity. This was generous provision by its founder, the former Lord Mayor of London Sir John Gresham (*c*.1496–1556), many comparable schools taking far fewer scholars. However the full complement of thirty was frequently not secured. The master would supplement his income by taking forty or fifty day boys and boarders; as fee-payers they outnumbered the free boys.

above **One of the many fine engravings by John Pine in John Holmes's text books for his pupils.**
[*Gresham's School Archive, ref. 2007.42*]

below **Part of the monument in Holt Church to Holmes and his wife Jane. Some of his books adorn the marble sculpture.**
[*photo Margaret Bird 2011*]

Enticing boys to their studies

The years 1729–60, under the inspirational John Holmes as master, had been an exciting time for the Holt schoolchildren, and much of Holmes's legacy lived on into the latter part of the century. He took immense pains over compiling and self-publishing large-print illustrated volumes to appeal to the boys; he also chose John Pine (1690–1756), then one of Britain's finest engravers, to prepare the illustrations for press. This was extremely unusual at a time when most schoolboys had to struggle with tiny print and no pictures at all.

below The Free Grammar School of 1554 faces the Market Place; its founder Sir John Gresham had been born in the predecessor of this Tudor manor house of Holt Pereers. The sketch of *c.*1717 is by the incoming master, a Scot, the Revd David Duncombe. It shows the schoolhouse known to Raven and William Hardy jnr when day boys 1781–83.   [*Gresham's School Archive, ref. 2012.9*]

left A replica of the arms of Sir John Gresham and the Fishmongers, the livery company in the City of London serving then and now as trustees. The panel adorns a side door today, but is seen in the sketch above the main entrance.   [*photo Margaret Bird 2022*]

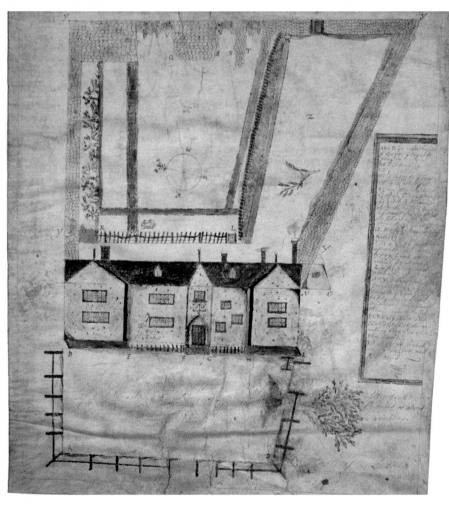

In one of his text books John Holmes (d.1760 aged 57) voiced his conviction that boys 'should be soothed and enticed to their studies' and not driven by harsh discipline; he was way ahead of his time in the field of child psychology. His fine memorial in the parish church also commemorates his wife Jane (d.1767 aged 70). She served as the school's matron, their epitaph stating that 'The children ever experienced in her a maternal tenderness.' Most unusually in public memorials the master's books are tied with a true lovers' knot to symbolise the strength of their marital partnership (pictured on page 23).

Holmes's pageants and masques, in which every child had a part, were continued under his equally humane successor James Smith (1725–94), who served as master for 26 years. He too understood the mindset of a young boy, as his fun English exercises demonstrate (below).[1]

The curriculum under both masters was unusually varied and lively: Latin, Greek (for those who wanted it), maths, French, geography, history, rhetoric, astronomy, surveying, merchant's accounts, navigation, bookkeeping and fine handwriting with flourishes. Parents like the Hardys wanted their sons to be prepared for life as active citizens ready for entry into the mercantile and commercial world; a narrow academic approach held no appeal for them. The playground at the front was open to the town, encouraging the boys' integration into adult life.

above **The 1555 school-house was demolished in 1858 and replaced with this building, now serving as the Gresham's Pre-Prep.** [*photo Margaret Bird 2022*]

[1] *masters* Holmes, Smith and their regimes are described in *Mary Hardy and her World*, vol. 1, pp. 410–28. The chapter on pupils has comparisons with other Norfolk schools at the time.

The study of Gresham's by Steve Benson and Martin Crossley Evans, *I Will Plant Me a Tree* (2002), has a wealth of information.

left **An amusing English exercise devised by James Smith. He has introduced deliberate mis-spellings for the boys to correct: eg 'a Meddow were we scate'.** [*Gresham's School Archive, ref. 2007.31*]

The A N S W E R.

Honoured Madam,

I Reseeved the Cake. and we have eat it before Twelfth-Day, which I am sometimes sorry for, but then I console my felf with the old Maxim, that, *One can't e t one's Cake and have it too.* O, niver fare my taken Care of my felf Mama; 'tis a Meddow were we fcate that's overflou'd, and not the River. Master *Sibthorpe* and I have fallen out, but Master *Henly* fend' his Complimants to you and my Pappa, together with my Duty, who am,

Honoured Madam,
Your dutiful and obedient Son,
ANTHONY FRANKLAND.

above **Eleven-year-old Mary Ann Hardy. Despite her large picture hat she is dressed for the playhouse, as are her parents in their portraits (pages 14 and 21).** [*by Huguier 1785: Cozens-Hardy Collection*]

below **Nelson House, south of the White Lion. Its name is misleading as the building has no direct connection with the famous admiral.** [*photo Margaret Bird 2022*]

Girls' education

Handsome Hanworth House [20] may well have been an institution rather than a private house. According to notices in the *Norwich Mercury* in our period Miss Mary Alpe's day and boarding school for young ladies occupied 'a large and commodious house' in the area of the market place. It was a female world run by and for women, and becoming a schoolmistress was an attractive proposition for educated single women and widows.

Schools for girls were not endowed, unlike many boys' schools. Ownership changed rapidly as fortunes rose and fell, and the pupils had little consistent leadership. In the space of 26 years the Holt school was owned and led in turn by the Misses Mary and Priscilla Alpe, the young widow Frances Chase and two Misses Clements.

The mistresses and their female assistants taught needlework and English grammar. They turned to visiting masters to teach writing, arithmetic, drawing, music, dancing and French. Annual boarding fees at 12 guineas (£12.60) were modest in comparison with other schools for girls which could reach 24 and 30 guineas a year.

The affectionate, dutiful Mary Ann Hardy became a day girl at the Holt school as soon as the family moved to Letheringsett. However tensions soon arose. The diarist championed her daughter when Mary Alpe accused the child of stealing a needlework case. Mary Ann was then sent briefly to boarding school twelve miles away at Fakenham. Interestingly both the Hardy parents home-tutored their daughter during the winter months, exposing her to the rigours of boarding only in the warmer weather.

Dancing the night away

Parents in the Hardys' circle treated their offspring as cherished companions and included them in their social activities from the age of three. Children as young as ten would dance into the small hours at balls and prolonged Twelfth Night celebrations—then a children's festival. It was a good time to be a middle-class child.

6 · The town in wartime

Holt was an overwhelmingly Whig stronghold in a generally Whig area. The printed pollbook records the names and voting choices of the 35 men who journeyed from Holt to Norwich to cast their votes in the county poll during the general election of 1802. Just five voted for the sole Tory candidate, Colonel the Hon. John Wodehouse. Two votes were permitted in those days, with 31 from Holt voting for Sir Jacob Henry Astley, 5th Bt, and 28 for Thomas William Coke—both Whigs. Cley's eight electors all voted Whig, and only one of Blakeney's ten voters polled for Wodehouse.

During the early part of the American war 1775–83 and for some of the French Revolutionary War 1793–1801 the supporters of the Whigs tended to press for peace. The commercial class predominant in the Holt area yearned for an end to the hostilities which were damaging Britain's trade. However once the American conflict evolved into all-out war with France, Spain and Holland the mood changed, and even pro-peace Whigs were prepared to support their country's cause. Likewise the spectre of Boney in the Napoleonic War 1803–15 united most factions. Britons then pulled together to resist the combined might of France, Spain, Holland and Denmark.

This was the backdrop to the extraordinarily intense militarisation of Holt for nearly thirty years from 1781. One myth needs to be dispelled at the outset. England's hero Horatio, Lord Nelson had no known connection with the town, and there is no record of his calling there either as a schoolboy or as an adult. The naming of Nelson House [21] in his honour dates from modern times.[1]

Ninety soldiers in the town

As outlined on page 5, Norfolk stood on the northern extremity of the invasion coast. The military authorities considered it highly vulnerable to enemy attack, and in 1803 decreed that Holt as 'the most central place' in the

above **The Alpe sisters moved their girls' school from Hindolveston to Holt in 1778. Hanworth House, at 43 Bull Street and re-fronted in 1744, is a strong candidate for the school, which drew girls from a wide area and was crammed with four-poster beds.**

Three headmistresses died in the schoolhouse within seven years at the turn of the century, two being aged only 51 and 47. [*photo Margaret Bird 2022*]

[1] *Nelson House* Many years after Nelson's death in 1805 it was lived in by a Suckling cousin. Nelson's uncle William Suckling never lived there, being very active in London for most of Nelson's adult life as Deputy Head and then Head of the Board of Customs.

right Spectacular iron-
work. The innkeeper here
illuminated his sign for
the 1801 celebrations for
peace with France, but the
wind blew the lights out.
[*photo Margaret Bird 2011*]

below The same sign is lit
at Christmas more than
two centuries later, as part
of Holt's long tradition.
[*photo Christopher Bird
2014*]

¹ *military hub* TNA: PRO
WO 30/100, pp. 147–52, 20
December 1803. A brigade
of heavy guns was des-
patched, consisting of 12-
pounders and howitzers.

² *display* The Hardys
joined thousands of
spectators watching
cavalry exercises, field days
and regimental reviews
and welcoming the Royal
Artillery to Holt (*Mary
Hardy and her World*,
vol. 4, chapter 9).

north of the county should become an anti-invasion hub.
As in the 1790s, the town hosted mobile heavy artillery
manned by the Regulars, the idea being that it would be
pulled to any point on the coast coming under assault.[1] It
is no wonder the inns had massive stabling provision:
the King's Head had stalls for one hundred horses (*Norwich Mercury*, 3 December 1796, 7 January 1797).

Holt's townsfolk found themselves having to cope
with billeting large numbers of troops for seventeen
months on end, many being lodged in private homes.
There were no barracks in the area, and the military
camp under canvas at Weybourne was in use for only a
few summers. Mary Hardy noted ninety soldiers taking
up winter quarters at Holt in November 1799, at a time
when the total resident population was a little under a
thousand. Once the town was 'full of them' six had to be
billeted at the diminutive King's Head at Letheringsett.

One consequence of the Army's arrival was the daily
presence of firearms, a soldier committing suicide at
Holt in August 1781; he 'shot himself intentionally', in
Mary Hardy's phrase. On a happier note the military
would also fire cannon rounds for national celebrations.
For safety they chose the open ground of Spout Hills
[22], as on the King's birthday in 1804. Even the anti-war
Hardys could not resist the allure of military display.[2]

Holt had an infantry unit of Volunteers (akin to the Home Guard in the Second World War) in the American war and the Napoleonic War. When inspected in late 1803 the men—all civilians—were judged 'steady' and the drummers and fifers 'very good'. The best that could be said of the officers, who included (briefly) William Hardy junior, was that they were 'attentive and desirous to improve'. They carried Prussian arms (Lieut. Colonel Metzner's report in the Norfolk Record Office, MS 66, 67; he served in the King's German Legion).

The electorate of Holt might be strongly Whig in temperament, and thus ambivalent about the endless wars. Nevertheless they took pains to make the Regulars feel at home, laying on a ball for the officers in August 1795.

Dinners for the poor in the market place

The coming of peace was embraced joyously. As in other towns and villages, the ratepayers laid on celebrations which included a public dinner for the poor of roast beef and plum pudding, laid out on tables in Holt's market place; well-to-do citizens waited upon those feasting.

Mary Hardy records the dinners of April 1789 (on the recovery of the King's health) and November 1801 (on the short-lived truce with France), when first 500 and then 700 of Holt's poor were catered for. Women helped with organising the huge meals and also painted backlit transparencies illuminating windows and inn signs.

7 · The town at play

In an age with very few leisure hours granted to working people any opportunity for celebration was highly prized.

The playhouse behind the White Lion

Few towns had purpose-built theatres in this period. Instead the troupes of touring players had to adapt to whatever was on offer. At Holt a barn in the White Lion's

above **Two scenes from Le Sage's farce *The Devil on Two Sticks*, a firm favourite amongst Holt's theatre-goers.**
[*Author's collection*]

¹ *ass, balloon* Norwich *Mercury*, 8 January 1785.
    In Holt's Sessions Week special performances were laid on, coinciding with horse races and balls.

² *hours* Today's figure is derived from OECD data. See *Mary Hardy and her World*, vol. 2, pp. 19–48.
    For the tensions see also vol. 4, pp. 364–91.

above The Frambeck near the Old Rectory. The rector took some common land at enclosure for himself. [*photo Margaret Bird 2012*]

facing page The Frambeck on Spout Hills. In 1781 M.J. Armstrong noted that Holt had some good houses, 'but there is a want of water that renders those houses inconvenient.' Drinking water was carted into town from this spring, Holt having just three public pumps. [*photo Margaret Bird 2013*]

backyard would be fitted up for the winter season [23]. The companies owned by the actor–managers William Scraggs and David Fisher advertised their productions in the Norwich newspapers, Mary Hardy also recording the performances. Scraggs's hardworking troupe gave 58 performances in four months at Holt 1784–85.

The curtain rose at 6.15 or 6.30 and came down at midnight. The programme usually consisted of three items: a major work such as by Shakespeare, Marlowe, Sheridan, Goldsmith and the female playwright Susanna Centlivre, followed by a musical interlude and then a farce. Ballad operas by O'Keefe and Shield, and Bickerstaff and Arne, proved popular as music had to be included each night if the players were to be spared being classed as vagabonds by the magistrates licensing them. Players paid immense attention to sets and the wow factor. Scraggs rode an ass and then took off from the Holt stage in a hot-air balloon at a time when balloon fever gripped the nation.[1]

Gentry, working people and servants were present, also women with just their children or other women; their menfolk might attend on another night. When self-employed households were the norm it was common for one adult to stay behind to 'mind the shop'. The classes mingled easily, with little display of deference.

Holt Fair: the sole holiday time

Holt Fair was held on two fixed days a year (page 5). It was a godsend for the labouring class: the two days a year granted to them as a holiday—if they had a considerate master or mistress. No such concept as annual leave existed then, with the result that fairs were treasured as reunions and as opportunities to exchange news.

From the diaries of Mary Hardy and Henry Raven we can calculate that annual hours worked were well over double today's British average: 3700 hours, against 1670 hours in recent times. The Hardys imposed a long-hours culture on their workforce, enforcing it by strict labour discipline. Tensions would frequently arise at fair time.[2]

Open spaces: losses at enclosure

Until 1810 Holt was surrounded by 2227 acres of open-access commons and heaths, with the workhouse [24] and the gibbet sited on Holt Heath east of the church.[1] Fields, commons and heaths crowded very close to the edge of the town centre. It was an open countryside, with no dark canopy of trees. However such a landscape held grave dangers for those on foot and on horseback, as in deep snow they had no way of identifying where the roads, tracks and pits lay. People died in snowdrifts, and the Hardys' drayman was in peril in 1784 when he 'lost himself upon Holt Heath, the snow being so very deep'.[2]

Enclosure under Acts of Parliament in 1807 and 1809 changed everything. The largest landowners took the 2227 acres into private hands.[3] The race course, on an escarpment by the Norwich road (now Holt Country Park), was lost. A further 688 acres, including the built-up area of the town, was left unenclosed. The poor suffered badly, obtaining a very meagre allocation. Only 120 acres were granted to them for grazing and for gathering fuel such as brushwood and gorse, compared with their old ample provision on the heaths. They were now permitted to pasture only one animal each, including a horse. And they could no longer use Spout Hills for gathering fuel.[4]

The landscape known to Mary Hardy was to vanish.

[1] *gibbet* It is marked on William Faden's county map of 1797. Gibbets are not gallows (page 15). The workhouse still stands, in today's Pearson Road near Grove Lane.

[2] *snowdrifts* Mary Hardy records many such losses.

The Hardys' drayman James Cornwell nearly died returning from a beer delivery to Cromer just a week after another such incident (Diary 2, 10 and 2 February 1784).

[3] *private* New lords of the manor, Henry Dampier and Jeremiah Smith (almost certainly not resident at Holt), had bought the three lordships following the easy-going rector's death in 1804.

That rector's son, also Revd Joshua Smith, secured two acres for his rectory property in the 1810 enclosure award.

[4] *Spout Hills* At least the award, which names the pure stream as the Frambeck [25], enshrined the rights of the people of Holt to Spout Hills and Spouts Common '*for ever*'.

Dependence on the precious drinking water helped to secure this right for them.

above The obelisk at East Dereham, on a card postmarked 28 August 1913. It stood near the George Inn. [*Dereham Heritage Trust, detail*]

below The serifed typeface on Holt's obelisk. [*photo Margaret Bird 2011*]

[1] G. *Carthew* 'The Town We Live In: A lecture delivered to the East Dereham Mechanics' Institute' (published in London in 1857).

Postscript: a tale of two obelisks

The obelisk [26] on Obelisk Plain, west of the High Street, is the Holt Society's logo (see page 1). Stylistically the elegant pineapple-topped structure would appear to date from the late seventeenth or early eighteenth century.

It used to have a twin at the north end of the market place in East Dereham (since 1990 known officially as Dereham). The typeface for the mileages displayed on this obelisk was very different from Holt's, suggesting the distances were incised once each pillar had been set in place. As at Holt, Dereham's figures were accurate as measured from their final location and emphasise the town's role as a route-convergence point. Unlike Holt's, Dereham's was later transformed into a street lamp.

Although it was broken up in the Second World War the Dereham Obelisk is better documented than Holt's. The historian George Carthew stated in 1855 that it had been donated by Sir Edward Astley, 4th Bt; a label in the Dereham Museum confirms the date of the gift as 1768.[1]

An entry of 2013 on the Norfolk Heritage Explorer database (NHER 53134) states that the two structures had once been gate piers at the park entrance for Melton Constable Hall, long the seat of the Astley family. It adds that Dereham's obelisk was dismantled and thrown down a well in Ruthen Place. This statement is confirmed by an undated note on the back of a photograph in the Dereham Heritage Trust collection showing the well and pump next to Oldfield's furnishing and hardware shop on the west side of the market place, beside Dereham's Assembly Rooms.

Both structures may date from between 1664 and 1670, when Sir Jacob Astley, 1st Bt, built Melton Constable Hall. A century later Capability Brown landscaped the park, at which point Sir Edward may have regarded the gate piers as redundant. He chose to give one to Holt and the other to East Dereham in 1768—the year he became MP for Norfolk. As the mileages do not reflect distances from Melton they were not incised during the Astleys' ownership.